PARTIES
AROUND A
PUNCH
BOWL

PARTIES
AROUND A
PUNCH
BOWL

KIMBERLY SCHLEGEL WHITMAN

GIBBS SMITH
TO ENRICH AND INSPIRE HUMANKIND

FOR MY LITTLE ONES, JR AND MILLIE.

THANKS FOR TESTING SO MANY PUNCH AND TREAT RECIPES

AND FOR ALWAYS BEING THE LIFE OF THE PARTY.

———————————————

First Edition
18 19 20 21 22   5 4 3 2 1

Text © 2018 Kimberly Schlegel Whitman
Photograph credits:
© 2018 by JerSean Golatt, pages 2, 8, 11, 12, 14, 15, 16, 19, 26, 28, 30, 31, 32, 35, 46, 48, 49, 50, 51, 52, 53, 55, 56 (center, right), 58, 61, 62, 70, 73, 74, 75, 76, 77 (left), 78, 80, 81, 83, 87, 88, 90, 91, 92, 95, 96, 97, 98, 101, 102, 104, 106, 110
© 2018 by John Cain Sargent, pages 6, 20, 23, 24, 36, 38, 39, 41, 42, 45, 56 (left), 57, 64, 66, 67, 68, 69, 77 (right), 86, 107
© 2018 by Kelsey Foster Wilson, page 84
© 2018 by Kimberly Schlegel Whitman, page 109

Published by
Gibbs Smith
P.O. Box 667
Layton, Utah 84041

1.800.835.4993 orders
www.gibbs-smith.com

Designed by Rita Sowins Design

Gibbs Smith books are printed on paper produced from sustainable PEFC-certified forest/controlled wood source. Learn more at www.pefc.org.
Printed and bound in Hong Kong

Library of Congress Cataloging-in-Publication Data

Names: Whitman, Kimberly Schlegel, author.
Title: Parties around a punch bowl / Kimberly Schlegel Whitman.
Description: First edition. | Layton, Utah : Gibbs Smith, [2018]
Identifiers: LCCN 2017036335 | ISBN 9781423648901 (hardcover)
Subjects: LCSH: Punches (Beverages) | Punch bowls--History. | LCGFT: Cookbooks.
Classification: LCC TX817.P86 W45 2017 | DDC 641.87/4--dc23
LC record available at https://lccn.loc.gov/2017036335

CONTENTS

THE PUNCH BOWL IS BACK!

One of the best things about punch is that you can't mess it up! It is meant to be mixed together, tasted, adjusted, and added to during the party. If you run out of one ingredient during the course of the party, you can even substitute something else and send the flavor in a different delicious direction. Punch is an evolving concoction that continues to change until the party is over.

One of the most enjoyable things about planning a party with punch is choosing the bowl and cups. Using a punch bowl has wonderful benefits, from bringing people together to the ease it provides a hostess, who won't have to fill glasses on her own all night. I like to serve punch in small cups so that guests are required to make frequent trips to refill. It keeps the party moving!

Thinking back to special occasions in my childhood, I immediately think of the sparkly punch that I enjoyed. Family reunions, weddings, church get-togethers— the punch bowl was always there and I looked forward to it. Serving punch from a gorgeous glass bowl with a glass or silver ladle was a sweet yet practical way to serve a large gathering. The table with the bowl and cups was a fun place to say hi to an old friend or meet a new one. The punch bowl was perfect for any party. But somehow, as I grew up, these delicious mixed batches started to disappear. The punch bowl was rarely pulled out of the silver closet, while signature drinks and specialty cocktails started to appear.

After spending several decades in the cupboard, the punch bowl has made a sparkling comeback! And this time around, it has the added element of nostalgic charm. As a host, you will find that it relieves the hard work of constantly mixing drinks for your guests. As a guest, you will enjoy finding a natural gathering spot to start a new conversation. And let's remember that the small cups that sit alongside the punch bowl were originally designed to keep punch lovers from overindulging too quickly; there is still something to be said for that.

THE PUNCH BOWL THROUGH THE AGES

The punch bowl has a rich history filled with great stories of celebrations. Some social historians believe that it first showed up in India long before the English arrived there in the early seventeenth century. The first concoction was made from five ingredients: a spirit, sugar, lemon, water and spices or tea. It was referred to as *paanch,* which is Hindi for "five." In the early seventeenth century, the English sailors of the British East India Company brought the "punch" back to England.

It didn't take long for the punch to catch on in England and spread to other European countries. Ceramic, porcelain and silver punch bowls became popular serving pieces and gradually became more elaborate. Some had lids; others had decorative stands. Some had matching ladles and cups for serving. Many were made for specific celebrations of special occasions and included elaborate inscriptions to commemorate successes, similar to a trophy.

The popularity of punch in English society is obvious from this nineteenth-century observation in Robert Chambers's *Book of Days,* 1864:

The punch-bowl was an indispensable vessel in every house above the humblest class. And there were many kindly recollections connected with it, it being very frequently given as a present. No young married couple ever thought of buying a punch-bowl; it was always presented to them by a near-relative.

Just as today, there were occasions when hosts and hostesses got creative and found alternative vessels for serving their favorite punch recipes. There are rumors of even fountains, boats and bathtubs being used on grand occasions as far back as the seventeenth century.

Although today's celebrations might not be as large or as grand as those punch parties of the past, the camaraderie and festivity that surround the punch bowl have not waned. Today's parties around a punch bowl are filled with style, color and creativity. We use punch bowls to celebrate all types of occasions, from formal to casual, and we have even stretched the ways we use our punch bowls.

In the pages that follow are some of my favorite ideas for punch bowl parties, along with recipes and tips for throwing a lively, memorable party with the punch bowl as a centerpiece for the table and for gathering guests. My favorite punch recipes stem from the sparkling citrus punch I enjoyed at church and family gatherings as a young girl. I've played with punch concoctions over the years and am thrilled to share what I have learned. Each libation that includes alcohol also has an alcohol-free alternative. There are recipes for appetizers or sweet treats to serve with the punch.

FIVE BASIC ELEMENTS

At the heart of all punch recipes are five basic elements: alcohol, acid, sugar, spice and water. You can play with all of these in inclusion and strength to find a recipe that works for you. It only takes two of these elements to make a punch!

One of the great things about a punch is that the recipe is always loose—and that is *my* kind of recipe! It is really hard to mess up a punch. The idea is that as the evening goes on, the punch will evolve as you refresh it. You might start the evening heavier on the alcohol, and as the night moves on, you might give the juice a longer pour instead. It is okay to let it continue to change and let your guests enjoy the different variations.

SIMPLE SYRUP

Simple syrup is an extremely versatile ingredient that can be used in baking as well as crafting cocktails or punches. I use simple syrup to keep my baked goods moist and flavorful in addition to infusing a seamless sweet kick to drinks.

Why simple syrup? The answer is fairly simple. If you're looking to sweeten your drink, there are several options. One is to add sugar, but this will result in a grainy texture and you risk the sugar not being fully dissolved, thus creating a film at the bottom. Honey can be used as a natural sweetener, but again, it might not fully mix with the other components, or it will become a slightly thick texture in your drink.

The solution? Heat sugar and water together so the sugar completely dissolves. Simple syrup blends into whatever concoction you are making, and it also allows a seamless blending medium for any flavor infusion that you might want to include. Here is the method along with some ideas for infusions:

1 cup water
1 cup sugar

Bring equal parts water and sugar to a boil in a saucepan and stir until the sugar dissolves. Remove the pan from the heat.

This is where you can be creative and add in extra flavors if you want to shake it up! I suggest:

VANILLA SIMPLE SYRUP: Add 2 teaspoons vanilla extract to the hot mixture after boiling.

MINT SIMPLE SYRUP: Slap 5 sprigs of mint and place in the mixture while it is heating. Remove once cooled.

ROSEMARY SIMPLE SYRUP: Place 2 stalks of rosemary into the heated mixture before it boils, and leave until cooled.

LEMON SIMPLE SYRUP: Add either 1 teaspoon lemon extract or 2 tablespoons lemon juice to the hot mixture after boiling.

LIME SIMPLE SYRUP: Add 2 tablespoons lime juice to the hot mixture after boiling.

Experimenting is half the fun! Find your favorite vessel for punch, choose a luscious punch recipe and decide what to serve with it. Then get the party started!

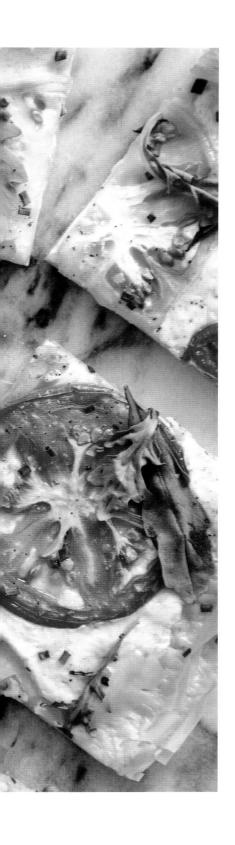

WARM
WEATHER
AL FRESCO

WHEN THE SUN STARTS TO BRING ITS WARMTH TO
OUR AREA, WE LOVE TO MOVE OUR ENTERTAINING
OUTDOORS. ONE OF MY HUSBAND'S FAVORITE THINGS
TO MAKE IS A RUM PUNCH THAT IS FILLED WITH
HIS FAVORITE FRUITS! WE LIKE TO SERVE IT WITH
A CROWD-PLEASING SAVORY TOMATO TART AND A
SWEET PINEAPPLE SPICE BAR.

JUSTIN'S RUM PUNCH

This refreshing fruity punch is perfect for a toasty al fresco lunch or an afternoon get-together. It is just the thing if you are having people over to take in a golf tournament on television or for socializing poolside. The gents love it as much as the ladies, but be warned—it is very potent! My husband Justin came up with this delicious punch recipe based on his friend Xan Moore's amazing cocktails!

2 apples
2 pears
3 limes
2 oranges
I (6-ounce) container
    blueberries
I pound strawberries, hulled

2 tablespoons grenadine
8 ounces light rum
8 ounces aged dark rum
8 ounces fresh-squeezed orange
    juice, chilled
6 ounces pineapple juice, chilled
2 1/2 ounces fresh lime juice
    (about 3 limes)

SERVES 16

TO MAKE KING-SIZE ICE CUBES:

The night before serving, prepare the fruit and make ice cubes:

Dice the apples and pears.

Slice the limes and oranges and then cut into quarters.

In king-size silicone ice cube trays, place a variety of diced apples and pears, blueberries, and strawberries. Add 1 piece of both orange and lime (leave, these sticking out).

Fill the tray with water, drowning the fruit completely except for the citrus wedges that stick out. Freeze overnight. Refrigerate remaining fruit.

TO MAKE THE PUNCH:

Mix the grenadine, light rum, aged dark rum, orange juice, pineapple juice, and lime juice in a large punch bowl. Stir with a wooden spoon.

Add in remaining fruit and stir gently.

Just before serving, add the fruit-filled ice cubes.

Use a large ladle to serve in old-fashioned-glasses, making sure each glass has diced fruit as well.

SAVORY TOMATO TART

I love to serve my guests comfort food, and this take on a tart is just that. I guess you could call it the cousin to a pizza, but the buttery and flaky phyllo dough makes it feel fancy!

I cup chopped onion

2 tablespoons minced garlic

2 tablespoons olive oil

3 sheets phyllo dough

I/3 cup melted butter or olive oil, for brushing

I cup grated mozzarella cheese

I cup grated Swiss cheese, divided

4 tomatoes, sliced

I egg

I/4 cup milk

IO basil leaves

MAKES A 9 X I3-INCH TART

In a large skillet, sauté the onion and garlic in olive oil until onion is translucent. Set aside.

Preheat oven to 400° F. Layer the phyllo sheets flat in a jelly roll pan, brushing the top of each sheet with butter or olive oil. Sprinkle the mozzarella and Swiss cheeses over the pie crust, reserving $1/4$ cup cheese. Next, spread on the onion and garlic mixture. Then place tomato slices side by side, covering the tart completely with tomatoes.

Whisk the egg and milk together and paint the edges of the tart with this mixture. Sprinkle the remaining $1/4$ cup of cheese over the tomatoes and bake for 18 to 20 minutes. Remove tart from the oven and sprinkle the basil leaves over the tart. Cut into mini squares.

TIPS

• This tart is extremely easy and very versatile. At the end of a long week, when you don't know what to do with your leftover tomatoes, this tart is the perfect answer for a supper at home.

• Don't be afraid to try different cheeses if Swiss isn't your favorite.

• Use any variety of tomatoes with this tart.

• For an alternative that is more pick-up friendly, try filling phyllo shells with the ingredients instead of layering phyllo sheets.

PINEAPPLE SPICE BARS

I have many happy recollections of my grandmothers opening Tupperware containers filled with a variety of "squares" that they would set out on beautiful silver trays or tiered tea stands. I had so many favorites and loved their small size and precise cuts because I knew that I could sample a few! For an adult party, the Rum Glaze is a scrumptious alternative.

3/4 cup white sugar
3/4 cup shortening
1/4 cup crushed pineapple
1/4 cup molasses
1 egg
2 teaspoons baking soda
1 teaspoon cinnamon
2 teaspoons ginger
1 teaspoon ground cloves
2 1/2 cups all-purpose flour
1/4 teaspoon salt

GLAZE:

1/4 cup butter
1/2 cup packed brown sugar
3 tablespoons milk
1 cup confectioners' sugar
1 teaspoon vanilla

RUM GLAZE:

1 cup confectioners' sugar
1/4 cup dark rum
Grated zest of 1 lemon

MAKES A 9 X 13-INCH PAN,
OR THINNER BARS IN A JELLY
ROLL PAN

Preheat oven to 350° F.

In a bowl, cream the sugar and shortening together. Stir in the crushed pineapple and molasses. Add the egg, beating well.

Mix the soda, spices, flour, and salt together in a separate bowl, then add the dry ingredients to the wet ingredients. If your mixture appears too dry, add a scant amount of milk until just moistened. Spread batter into a 9 x 13-inch pan (for thicker bars) or a jelly roll pan (for thinner bites). Bake for 15 minutes, or until cooked through. Remove from oven and let cool about 1 hour before glazing with one of the two options.

FOR THE GLAZE, melt the butter, brown sugar, and milk together over medium heat, whisking constantly until mixture begins to boil. Remove from heat and let cool for 10 minutes. Add confectioners' sugar and vanilla; whisk until smooth. Pour glaze over the cake, adjusting the thickness of the glaze by adding milk or confectioners' sugar as needed.

FOR THE RUM GLAZE, mix all ingredients until you have a pourable glaze. Drizzle over the spice bars.

TIP

• For an extra flavor of the islands, try adding 2 teaspoons of dark rum to the bar recipe along with the wet ingredients.

• These bars are an easy transition into fall and Christmas if you substitute the pineapple for brown sugar.

• We like our bars extra soft. For a firmer bar, bake a bit longer.

• If you don't have a strong sweet tooth, I recommend the thinner Rum Glaze alternative, which includes an extra kick.

• Flowers stuck into a leafy pineapple top makes a festive decoration.

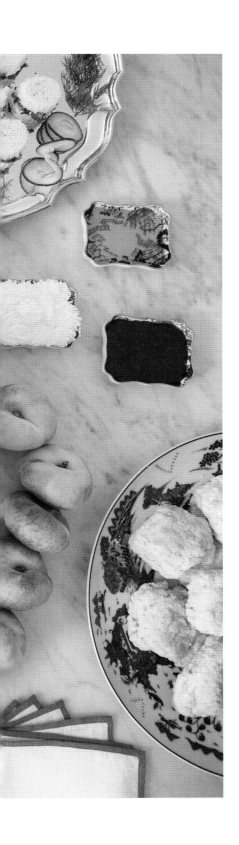

SOUTHERN HIGH TEA

WHO SAID HIGH TEA CAN'T INVOLVE A PUNCH BOWL? WE'VE ADAPTED ONE OF OUR FAVORITE PUNCH RECIPES TO FIT TEA TIME PERFECTLY! PAIR IT WITH A DECADENT PILE OF SCONES, CLOTTED CREAM AND JAM AND YOU REALLY CAN'T GO WRONG. THIS MENU IS GREAT FOR ANY AFTERNOON GET-TOGETHER FOR FAMILY OR FRIENDS. IT IS A FESTIVE TWIST ON A TRADITIONAL TEA-TIME TREAT. SAVE THE LEFTOVERS AND ENJOY THEM THE NEXT DAY!

PEACH TEA PUNCH

Whether you want to take the easy route or go all out with a true tea, your guests will love these fresh takes on teatime. Line your punch bowl with tea cups instead of glasses and let your guests indulge in one of these refreshing afternoon treats. Freeze your peach tea ice cubes ahead of time.

PEACH TEA THE LONG WAY:

7 bags peach tea, brewed according to package
  directions
2 cups sugar
1 liter sparkling lemonade
1 liter ginger ale
Peach tea ice cubes
Sliced peaches, for garnish, optional

MAKES 25 SERVINGS

After brewing the tea, stir in the sugar until it dissolves; let the tea cool completely. Into your punch bowl, pour the cooled tea, lemonade, and ginger ale. Add peach tea ice cubes. Garnish with beautiful peach slices if desired. Ladle punch into cups and serve.

TIP FOR JULEPS:

If you want to create a twist on this classic tea, I suggest transforming it into Peach Juleps. Add bourbon to this southern treat and use fresh sprigs of mint for garnish. You will have arrived in the Deep South!

PEACH TEA THE EASY STREET:

The first method is true tea, but when you are in a pinch, this method is a great go-to!

2 packets Crystal Light peach tea
2 packets Crystal Light lemonade
2 liters ginger ale*
2 (16-ounce) bottles sparkling mineral water (I like
  Topo Chico)

MAKES 25 SERVINGS

Stir all ingredients together, pour into a punch bowl, add ice, and serve!

*To reduce the amount of sugar, substitute sparkling water for the ginger ale.

HOMEMADE SCOTTISH SCONES

Scotland is famous for it's fluffy, dense scones. I promise, once you have tasted one you will crave more! Even though many of Scotland's most famous tea houses keep their scone recipes tightly guarded, I think this one gets as close as they come! Serve it with your favorite jam and some clotted cream at tea time, but be sure to make extra, as you will want to have more for breakfast the next morning!

2 cups all-purpose flour

1/2 cup sugar

4 teaspoons baking powder

6 tablespoons cold butter

1/2 cup sour cream

1/2 cup buttermilk

1 tablespoon vanilla, mixed into the buttermilk

1 egg, beaten

Clotted cream or butter, for serving

Favorite jams, for serving

MAKES 25 MINI SCONES   OR 15 LARGE SCONES

In a large bowl, place the flour, sugar, and baking powder. Cut in the butter until the mixture is completely blended. Make a well in the dough and add the sour cream and buttermilk with vanilla. Mix until a dough forms. Do not overhandle.

Preheat oven to 350° F.

On a lightly floured surface, press the dough out flat with your hands (do not use a rolling pin) and use a biscuit cutter to cut the dough into small rounds. Brush the rounds with the beaten egg. Bake for 15 minutes, or until baked through and brown on top.

Serve with clotted cream or butter and your favorite jams.

TIPS:

• Always use cold butter.

• Do not overwork the dough or your scones will be tough.

• Make a savory or sweet scone by adding your favorite ingredients. I like adding fruit, chocolate chips, and cinnamon sugar.

• If you end up with leftovers, try one of these suggestions:

» Freeze them and pull out for your next overnight guests.

» Use them in a trifle.

» Put them in a food processor, process to crumbs, mix with melted butter, and make a crust or crumble for a cobbler or tart.

EASTER EGG HUNT

OUR ANNUAL EASTER EGG HUNT IS ONE OF MY FAVORITE EVENTS TO PLAN. WE LOVE TO INVITE OUR FRIENDS TO WHITE OAKS RANCH AND ENJOY THE OUTDOORS. MY UNCLE BRINGS A GALVANIZED TUB FULL OF BABY CHICKS FOR THE CHILDREN TO SEE BEFORE WE GATHER TOGETHER AND ASK AN HONORED GUEST TO READ THE BIBLICAL EASTER STORY. AFTER THE STORY, THE HUNTING BEGINS AND OUR LITTLE GUESTS GATHER ON THE FRONT LAWN TO FIND THE TREASURES HIDDEN BEHIND THE TREES AND IN THE BUSHES. THIS YEAR, OUR SEVENTH ANNUAL HUNT, CALLED FOR A PUNCH THAT WOULD BE AS BRIGHT AS OUR DECORATIONS AND TREATS THAT WOULD PLEASE THE LITTLE EGG-HUNTERS IN ATTENDANCE.

PINEAPPLE-LIME PUNCH

2 (12-ounce) cans frozen limeade
  concentrate
4 cups pineapple juice
1/4 cup lime juice
1 liter ginger ale
1 (25-ounce) bottle Prosecco

MAKES 16 SERVINGS

Refrigerate all ingredients for 8 hours or overnight. When ready to party, combine all ingredients in your favorite punch bowl.

TIPS:

• For a stronger punch, add rum.

• For a nonalcoholic punch, omit the Prosecco and add sparkling limeade.

• Make lime ice cubes by freezing lime juice in your favorite ice mold.

MACAROON NESTS

I egg white

1/8 teaspoon salt

I teaspoon vanilla

I teaspoon rum, optional

2/3 cup sweetened condensed
  milk

3 3/4 cups sweetened flaked
  coconut

1/2 cup white icing

70–90 jelly beans

MAKES 24

Preheat oven to 300° F. Spray a 24-cup mini muffin pan with cooking spray and set the pan aside. (I like Pam Baking No-Stick Cooking Spray, as it has flour in it.)

In a large bowl, combine the egg white, salt, vanilla, rum, and sweetened condensed milk. Then carefully mix in the coconut.

Using a small melon baller, scoop 2 tablespoons of the coconut mixture into each muffin cup. Lightly press the mixture into the bottom and up the sides of each cup, using your thumb or the back of a small spoon. Bake for 20 minutes, or until nests are golden on the top. Remove nests from muffin tin and cool.

After nests have cooled completely, use a piping bag (or plastic bag with a corner cut off) to pipe a small amount of icing into each nest. Add 2 or 3 jelly bean eggs and press them gently so that they stay.

PEEPS RACERS

Make dessert sweet with these charming treats. I just love these—always a hit with the little ones! The cars are made with Twinkies, vanilla cookies, yogurt pretzels and bunny Peeps.

12 single Twinkies
48 small round vanilla cookies
White icing, in a piping bag
12 bunny Peeps
12 yogurt-covered pretzels

MAKES 12

Using a paring knife, carve out a 3/4-inch V shape in each Twinkie, about three quarters of the way back.

For the wheels, pipe a small dob of icing near the front and back on each side of the Twinkie. Press a small vanilla cookie onto each of the four dobs (posed as wheels).

If needed, pipe some icing into the bottom and edges of the V, and place a bunny Peeps (posed as driver) and a pretzel (upside down, posed as steering wheel) in the Twinkie. (If the Twinkie filling will hold the Peeps in place, you don't need to add the icing.)

AVOCADO DEVILED EGGS

These colorful "Easter eggs" are a fun twist on the classic deviled egg. Their festive colors and easy flavor make them crowd pleasers, perfect for a large gathering or an easy selection to take to a potluck.

2 large avocados, halved and
  flesh moved to a bowl
6 hard-boiled eggs, halved and
  yolks moved to a bowl
1/4 cup chopped mango
3 teaspoons lime juice
3 teaspoons lemon juice
1 teaspoon garlic salt
Pepper
Paprika, optional garnish

MAKES 12

Mash avocado and egg yolks together, then mix with mango, lime and lemon juice, garlic salt, and pepper to taste.

Fill each egg half with this mixture. (I use a piping bag to create a beautiful whipped texture.) Sprinkle a little paprika on each half.

TIPS:

• The lemon juice keeps the mixture from discoloring.

• Crumbled crispy bacon makes a tasty extra topping.

• If you want to dye the egg whites, fill three bowls with about 1 cup water each. To each bowl, add 4 to 6 drops of either red, blue, or green liquid food coloring, or a blend of your choice. Soak egg white halves in the colored water in the refrigerator. The colors become more saturated after a few hours, but you can make them lighter shades by using less food coloring or deeper shades by using more. Remove egg whites from the dye cups and let drain in paper towels.

— Decorate with Cabbage Vases —

Our annual Easter Egg Hunt is always held outdoors, which means that sometimes the weather doesn't want to cooperate (and occasionally rains us out!). We are always trying to come up with table centerpieces that will hold up to windy days or humidity. When the talented Shannon King of Hope Hill Designs suggested we use cabbages as vases, I was thrilled! The cabbages were heavy enough that they stayed put, and the flowers were positioned close enough to the cabbage vase that I didn't have to worry about them moving around in the wind.

Here is how to make your own cabbage vase:

1. Choose a cabbage and choose a square floral oasis that will fit in a hollowed-out square. Soak the oasis in water for several hours.

2. Meanwhile, figure out how the cabbage stands upright. You may need to shave off part of base to aid this. Use a sharp flat knife.

3. Determine where you would like flowers to be placed in the cabbage. (I placed some at an angle and others directly in the center.)

4. Remove any damaged outer leaves and then pull a few exposed fresh leaves a quarter to halfway down to add dimension to you arrangement.

5. Using a sharp, sturdy kitchen knife, cut a square in the top of the cabbage. Then cut into the square in a crisscross fashion and hollow out the cabbage.

6. Cut and place your presoaked floral oasis in the square and make sure the oasis lays flat, in line with the cabbage.

7. Insert gorgeous fresh-cut blooms. I like using stems of smaller blooms as opposed to, say, large hydrangea heads. This gives the arrangement some height and preserves the full effect of the cabbage. I choose one color family per arrangement, but you might like to mix colors.

LEMON TWIST AFTERNOON

DAY OR NIGHT, THIS CITRUS PUNCH WORKS AT ANY TYPE OF GET-TOGETHER. WHETHER HOSTING A FORMAL TEA PARTY OR GATHERING FRIENDS FOR A REGULAR BOOK CLUB, A BOWL OF PUNCH CAN BE THE PERFECT THING TO DELIGHT YOUR GUESTS. ADD AN EASY BUNDT CAKE AND TEA BAG COOKIES, AND YOU HAVE AN EASY MENU TO MAKE A GATHERING SPECIAL.

LEMONADE PUNCH

2 (12-ounce) cans frozen
lemonade concentrate
1 (12-ounce) can frozen pineapple
concentrate
1 liter ginger ale
4 cups sparkling water
1/2 cup lemon juice

SERVES 16

Mix all ingredients together. Add garnishes and serve.

TIPS:

• The frozen concentrate will keep the punch cool as it thaws, which means you don't necessarily need ice unless you want to make a pretty ice ring.

• You can always substitute the sparkling water with sparkling lemonade.

• Sliced lemon and a few mint leaves make pretty garnishes.

• For an adult beverage, you could add 1 cup of vodka.

• Use this as a base recipe and then to branch out. The beauty of punch is that you can make it your own. Try adding other fruits or garnishes from the Garnish Guide (page 105).

CITRUS BUNDT CAKE

THE LONG WAY:

3 cups flour
1 cup white sugar
1/2 cup brown sugar
2 teaspoons baking powder
3/4 teaspoon sea salt
3 lemons
2 small oranges
1 cup sour cream
6 large eggs
1 1/2 sticks butter, melted
Lemon Simple Syrup (see page 10), optional

Preheat oven to 325° F. Spray a Bundt pan with baking spray and set aside.

Sift the flour, sugars, baking powder, and salt into a bowl. Grate the zest from the lemons and oranges and mix zest into the flour mixture.

Remove all of the bitter white pith from the lemons and oranges. Squeeze the juice from the lemons and oranges into a bowl; then cut the fruits into segments and place these in another bowl. Reserve the juice.

Add the sour cream to the flour mixture; then add the eggs one at a time, beating after each addition until mixed. Now beat in the melted butter and citrus juice. Once this is well mixed, add in the segments and mix well. Pour batter into the greased pan. Bake for about 40 minutes and test for doneness; if not cooked through, check again in 10 minutes.* Be careful not to let the cake burn. Let cake cool.

Pour cooled Lemon Simple Syrup over the finished cake. This will ensure a moist cake while giving it an extra layer of flavor.

* It is important to know your oven. Some ovens cook faster than others and you can risk burning your beautiful cake!

THE SHORT CUT:

1 box lemon cake mix
1 cup sour cream
4 eggs
1/4 cup orange juice
1/4 cup lemon juice
1 cup oil
2 teaspoons lemon zest
2 teaspoons orange zest
Lemon Glaze, optional

Preheat oven to 325° F. Spray a Bundt pan with baking spray and set aside.

Place the cake mix, sour cream, eggs, juices, oil, and zest in the bowl of a stand mixer and mix well. Pour batter into the Bundt pan and bake for 45 minutes, or until cooked through. Let cake cool and then transfer to a cake stand. Make the glaze and drizzle over the cake.

Lemon Glaze:

2 cups confectioners' sugar
1/4 cup lemon juice

TIPS:

• While the long way makes a more traditional pound cake, I love the ease of the short cut! Either way will give you all the citrus you've been craving.

• The simple syrup and the glaze are optional and can be used on either recipe.

• Garnish with lemon or orange slices.

• A well-greased pan is your best friend when it comes to pound cakes. Take the time on the front end to ensure it goes your way!

• For the simple syrup, I recommend transferring it into a squeeze bottle to make your pouring even and consistent.

CROWN CUPCAKES

I box white cake mix

I cup sugar

I cup all-purpose flour

4 egg whites

I cup sour cream

1/2 cup sweetened condensed
   milk

1/2 cup water

2 tablespoons oil

I tablespoon vanilla bean paste

VANILLA ICING:

I stick unsalted butter, softened

4 cups powdered sugar

I tablespoon vanilla*

1/4 cup whole milk, plus more if
   needed

MAKES 24

Preheat oven to 350° F. Line a regular-size cupcake pan with your choice of cupcake liners.

Mix the cake mix, sugar, and flour together using a stand mixer. Add the egg whites in three or four additions, beating well after each addition. Then add the sour cream, condensed milk, water, and oil. Finally, add the vanilla bean paste.

Fill each cupcake liner three-fourths of the way full with the batter. Bake for 12 to 15 minutes, or until cooked through.

FOR THE ICING:

Beat the butter and powdered sugar together. Add the vanilla and milk and beat until the icing reaches the desired consistency. The icing should be spreadable but not too thin. Add a little extra milk if you need to. To thicken your icing, add a little more powdered sugar.

FOR THE CROWNS:

Top off the cupcake with a paper crown. I used a classic paper doily for this. Carefully cut off the outside edge of the doily, spray it with a touch of edible gold cake decorating spray, and wrap it end-to-end to make a crown. To help it keep its round shape, add a small drop of icing to one end and attach it to the other; the icing works almost like a glue. Place the crown on top of the cupcake for an elegant extra touch.

* To preserve the white look of the icing, use clear vanilla.

BEST-EVER SUGAR COOKIES

I stick unsalted butter

I cup sugar

I tablespoon vanilla extract

2 tablespoons Frangelico liqueur

2 teaspoons almond extract

I egg

2 cups all-purpose flour

I tablespoon baking powder

I teaspoon salt

MAKES 12 TEA BAG–SHAPED COOKIES

Cream the butter and sugar together. Add the three flavorings and the egg.

In a separate bowl, combine the flour, baking powder, and salt. Add this to the wet mixture. Beat just until combined. Refrigerate for 1 hour.

Preheat oven to 350° F.

Roll out cookie dough on a lightly floured surface to a thickness of about $^1/_4$ inch. Cut out desired shapes using a cookie cutter or knife and, if making tea bag shapes, cut out a small hole using the tip of a straw. Transfer cookies to a baking sheet. Bake for 9 minutes. Do not overbake.

After cookies have cooled, apply the chocolate dip or royal icing.

CHOCOLATE DIP

I (24-ounce) package chocolate almond bark

12 pieces of string about 5 inches long

Place the chocolate almond bark in a microwave safe bowl and microwave for 2-minute increments until the chocolate is a smooth consistency. Lay out waxed paper on a work surface where the cookies will dry.

Dip each cookie into the melted chocolate and lay it on the waxed paper to dry thoroughly.

If making tea bag cookies, once the cookies are dry, loop a piece of string through the hole in the top of each cookie to complete the effect!

Royal icing is a delicious alternative to chocolate dip for other cookie shapes.

ROYAL ICING

2 egg whites

I cup confectioners' sugar

Whisk egg whites until soft peaks form. Add confectioners' sugar to mixture and continue to whisk until well blended. Increase confectioners' sugar if stiffer icing is desired.

COOKIE DECORATING TIPS:

• If you are hosting a seated event and making tea bag–shaped cookies, you might attach a small flag of paper to the tea bag string to serve as your place card.

SUMMER FRESH PICNIC

SINCE A LOT OF MY ENTERTAINING IS DONE FOR FAMILY, AND SINCE ONE OF MY SISTERS AND I HAVE YOUNG CHILDREN, I AM ALWAYS LOOKING FOR A PARTY MENU THAT WILL APPEAL TO A WIDE RANGE OF AGES— FROM TODDLERS TO GRANDPARENTS. WHEN I COME UP WITH RECIPES THAT EVERYONE LIKES, I AM SO HAPPY TO HAVE FOUND A WINNER!

MY CHILDREN LIKE TO BE IN PARTY PLANNING MODE WITH ME. MY SON'S SPECIALTY IS RESEARCHING IDEAS, AND MY DAUGHTER LIKES TO BE IN THE KITCHEN. THEY BOTH LOVE A GOOD PROJECT, SO PUTTING THEM TO WORK ON HOLLOWING OUT A WATERMELON IS ALWAYS A WELCOME CHORE! IT IS IMPORTANT WHEN ENTERTAINING A WIDE VARIETY OF AGES TO PUT AS MUCH THOUGHT INTO THE PRESENTATION OF THE PUNCH AND FOOD INTENDED FOR THE YOUNGER SET AS FOR THE GROWN-UPS! WHAT CHILD DOESN'T LIKE TO OOH AND AHH OVER A COLORFUL DRINK OR EAT FRUIT OFF A LOLLIPOP-LIKE SKEWER? I KNOW MINE DO!

KICKY WATERMELON PUNCH

1 large watermelon, reserving
   melon balls
1 (25-ounce) bottle raspberry
   Bellini (I use Trader Joe's)
1 (64-ounce) bottle Watermelon
   Cooler
1 (20-ounce) bottle sparkling
   mineral water (I like Topo
   Chico)
1 (33-ounce) bottle sparkling
   limeade
Limes and oranges, sliced, for
   garnish

SERVES 25–30*

Lay the watermelon on its side and cut off the top fourth of the stem-end of the melon. Then begin carving out the inside of the melon. (Be careful not to puncture the sides or bottom of the watermelon or you will have quite the mess on your hands when you pour in the punch!) I like using a Parisienne scoop for making small watermelon balls, which I freeze and use later to keep the punch cool and add as a garnish. Once you have completely removed the inside of the watermelon, pour all the liquid ingredients into the carved-out watermelon punch bowl.

Add the frozen melon balls as desired. Float the lime and orange slices in the bowl for a pretty effect.

* The watermelon can only hold so much, but the recipe will serve more than the melon can hold.

TIPS:

• With the leftover watermelon, I make a purée in the food processor, adding a little lime juice and a pinch of sugar. I either add it to the punch or freeze it as pops. Kids really like it!

• As with all punches, this one is flexible. If you want a stronger punch, add your favorite liquor, such as vodka or tequila.

• For a kid-friendly twist, leave out the Bellini and add lemonade and/or the watermelon purée.

JR'S FAVORITE PUNCH

I keep a pitcher of this at home almost all of the time, as my son, JR, loves to have it after school or as a refreshment while playing outside.

3 cups ginger ale, cold
2 cups orange juice, cold
2 cups pineapple juice, cold

MAKES 2 QUARTS

Mix all liquids together in a large pitcher, stir and serve!

If you have too much, pour extra into ice cube trays and serve them with this punch so that the water in regular ice cubes doesn't dilute the mixture.

If you want to cut down on the sugar, substitute sparkling mineral water (Topo Chico is my go-to brand) for the ginger ale.

TIP FOR LEFTOVER PUNCH:

• I love to pour the leftover punch into ice pop molds and freeze for my kids to enjoy later!

MINTED FRUIT SKEWERS

Whether having friends over to swim or getting ready for a larger get-together, I often turn to no-cook recipes like this one. I like the simplicity of the refreshing fruit and the exotic mix of mint presented in a way that feels both fun and thoughtful. These easy skewers are a hit with guests of all ages!

Watermelon, cut into bite-size pieces
Pineapple, cut into bite-size pieces
Strawberries
Blueberries
Mint leaves

Thread pieces of fruit onto skewers, alternating with mint leaves. Stand the skewers in mint julep cups for a stunning presentation!

TIPS:

• Offer all the extra fruit in bowls along with Strawberry Fruit Dip.

• Use your mint julep cups all year-round: decorate for fall and Christmas with this same technique. Establish a base at the bottom and make pretty flower arrangements.

• Mint julep cups are a perfect way to present your favorite veggies and their complementary dip: a little dip in the bottom will hold your tall veggies in place until eaten.

STRAWBERRY FRUIT DIP

1 small carton vanilla Greek yogurt
1 small carton strawberry Greek yogurt
2 tablespoons honey
1/4 cup strawberry jam

Combine all ingredients together. Keep refrigerated until just before serving.

TIP FOR STABILIZING:

• Cut the top off a large strawberry to create a flat side; then place the strawberry flat side down in the bottom of a mint julep cup. When you place the skewers in the cup, pierce the strawberry with them to give them a stable base.

JAR SALADS

Be sure to use wide-mouth jars. Put in the wet ingredients first, then layer other ingredients, with the dry ingredients on top. Jar salads are great for any event, but especially those where your partygoers can come and go. They can either eat their salad at the party or take it on the run! I have sent plenty of guests out the door with a jar of salad and a fork tied to the top with a ribbon!

VEGGIE LOVER'S SALAD WITH BALSAMIC–LIME VINAIGRETTE

Balsamic–Lime Vinaigrette (recipe right)
Cucumbers
Riced cauliflower
Riced broccoli
Black beans
Bell peppers
Sunflower seeds
Spinach lettuce
Shaved Parmesan cheese

Add the above ingredients to individual jars in the order listed. Salad ingredients can be changed to whatever you are craving.

With any version of the jar salad, the order of assembly is extremely important! You begin with the dressing and the wet ingredients—fruit, tomatoes, anything that has excess moisture. After the wet ingredients, you add quinoa or beans. This will create a nice barrier between the wet ingredients and the other ingredients.

Following the beans, you then put in your moisture-resistant ingredients—broccoli, carrots, etc.

Next, add your protein, croutons, nuts, etc.

Lastly, put the lettuce on top and sprinkle on any cheese the recipe calls for. Leave a little room between the top of the salad and the top of the jar so that when you shake it, all the ingredients will mix evenly.

Balsamic–Lime Vinaigrette

1 cup balsamic vinegar
1/4 cup olive oil
1/4 cup lime juice
1/4 teaspoon ground black pepper
1/8 teaspoon garlic salt

Place all ingredients in a small jar and shake.

SOUTHWEST SALAD WITH LIME VINAIGRETTE

Italian Lime Vinaigrette
Black beans
Corn, fresh-cooked or roasted, cut off the cob
Quinoa
Carrots, grated
Romaine and Spinach leaves
1 tablespoon three-cheese blend

Lime Vinaigrette

4 tablespoons fresh-squeezed lime juice
2 tablespoons fresh-squeezed orange juice
1 tablespoon sugar
2 tablespoons canola oil
1 teaspoon seasoned salt
Seasoned salt
Pepper

In a small bowl whisk together the lime juice, orange juice, and sugar until the sugar has dissolved. Slowly add the oil in a stream, whisking to emulsify. Season with seasoned salt and pepper to taste.

TRADITIONAL SALAD WITH ITALIAN VINAIGRETTE

Italian Vinaigrette with Herbs
Tomatoes
Quinoa
Carrots
Broccoli
Avocado
Romaine and spinach blend
Three-cheese blend

Italian Vinaigrette with Fresh Herbs

2 tablespoons red wine vinegar
I teaspoon apple cider vinegar
I shallot, minced
I tablespoon freshly squeezed lemon juice
1/2 clove garlic, minced or mashed to a paste
6 tablespoons extra virgin olive oil
I teaspoon coarsely chopped fresh oregano leaves
2 fresh basil leaves, coarsely chopped
Salt and pepper

In a small bowl, whisk together the vinegars, shallot, lemon juice, and garlic. Slowly add the olive oil in a stream, whisking to emulsify. Stir in the oregano and basil. Season with salt and pepper to taste.

FRUIT LOVER'S SALAD WITH RASPBERRY VINAIGRETTE

Raspberry Vinaigrette
Blueberries, raspberries, and strawberries
Craisins
Quinoa
Slice almonds
Baby kale and spinach
Feta cheese, crumbled

Raspberry Vinaigrette

3 tablespoons raspberry balsamic vinegar
I tablespoon fresh-squeezed lemon juice
5 tablespoons canola oil
4 fresh raspberries, mashed
Salt and pepper

Combine the vinegar and lemon juice. Whisk constantly while adding the oil in a steady stream; whisk until emulsified. Stir the mashed raspberries into the dressing. Season with salt and pepper to taste.

CUCUMBER–WATERMELON SALAD WITH RASPBERRY MERLOT DRESSING

Bolthouse Raspberry Merlot Dressing*
Cucumber, chopped
Watermelon, diced
Spinach leaves
Feta cheese, crumbled
Sliced almonds

*Sweetened Balsamic Vinaigrette makes a nice dressing option.

Sweetened Balsamic Vinaigrette

2 tablespoons balsamic vinegar
2 teaspoons sugar
6 tablespoons extra virgin olive oil
Salt and pepper

Place vinegar in a small bowl and whisk in the sugar until dissolved. Slowly add the oil in a steady stream, whisking to emulsify. Season with salt and pepper to taste.

TIPS:

• For salads on the go, tie a fork to the top of the jar using a ribbon.

• Salad jars make an attractive tabletop presentation! If you are having a sit-down luncheon, allow the guests to choose which salad they want from your prepared jar options, return to their seats, shake it up, and pour it onto their plates. It's a great way to provide options without having to make big bowls of salads to choose from.

• Also perfect for picnics.

• For a more formal presentation, or if you want to keep salads on hand for house guests to eat at any time, assemble your favorite salads, and keep them in the refrigerator. When you are ready to serve, shake the jars, and pour the contents into a large salad bowl or onto individual plates to enjoy.

MARGARITA MIXER

LOOKING FOR A WAY TO ADD A LITTLE GLAMOR
TO YOUR REGULAR TACO TUESDAY? WHY NOT TRY
HOSTING A MARGARITA MIXER? THERE IS NO NEED TO
HIRE A FROZEN MARGARITA MACHINE OR TO STAND
BEHIND A TABLE MIXING MARGS FOR YOUR GUESTS ALL
NIGHT. INSTEAD, MAKE A BATCH OF MARGARITA PUNCH
AND SERVE IT ALONGSIDE MY TANGY MANGO TWIST
ON GUACAMOLE. STUFFED MINI BELL PEPPERS GO THE
DISTANCE TO KEEP YOUR GUESTS SATISFIED.

MARGARITA PUNCH

I 1/2 cups Casa Dragones Blanco tequila
I bottle lime margarita mix (I use Trader Joe's)
I bottle Mango Bellini (I use Trader Joe's)
I cup lime juice
1/2 cup simple syrup (see page 10)
16 ounces sparkling mineral water (Topo Chico)
Mango slices, for garnish
Lime slices, for garnish

SERVES 16

Mix all ingredients, except garnishes, together. Be sure to add the Topo Chico last, to preserve the fizz.

Garnish individual cups with slices of mango and/or lime.

TIPS:

• The classic lime margarita mix is a time-saving party shortcut!

• If you want to do it all from scratch, I suggest using your favorite margarita recipe and not being afraid to play with it until you love it!

• Take creative freedom: use this recipe as a base and go from there. If you don't want the mango twist, take it out. Just be sure to adjust your liquor amounts if you shift the other components.

VIRGIN MARGARITA PUNCH (PICTURED, RIGHT)

I (6-ounce) can frozen limeade concentrate
I (6-ounce) can frozen lemonade concentrate
I (25-ounce) bottle Welch's Sparkling Mango Bellini Juice (this brand is nonalcoholic)
Limes, for garnish

SERVES 10

Place the frozen concentrates in a large bowl and slowly pour the mango Bellini over the concentrates! Serve chilled and garnish with limes.

MOJITO PUNCH

4 cups light rum
I cup lime juice
4 cups sparkling mineral water
I bottle sparkling limeade
I cup simple syrup (see page 10)
1/2 cup muddled mint

SERVES 10 TO 12

Be sure all of your liquids are chilled. Combine all ingredients and pour into a punch bowl with ice. Serve with crushed ice.

TIPS

• A minted ice ring will keep this punch cold, and having the extra mint in the ice ring really does not overpower the flavor of the punch.

• If you don't like the limeade twist, you can substitute your favorite flavor, like lemonade or something else to add some tartness.

MANGO
GUACAMOLE

This slightly sweet and salty guacamole served with tortilla chips is a delectable theme pairing for Margarita Punch.

2 avocados

I mango

I/2 cup chopped onion

I/4 cup chopped cilantro

I teaspoon garlic salt

I/4 cup chopped fresh tomato

I/4 cup lime juice

MAKES ABOUT 3 CUPS

Combine all ingredients together and serve with tortilla chips.

— Stuffed Mini Bells —

If you are looking for a festive way to serve your dips, look no further than the mini bell pepper! I love this colorful addition to a tablescape. Slice the bell peppers in half lengthwise and fill with your favorite dips or fillings, such as chicken salad, pimento cheese, or guacamole.

If you want the guests to use chips with their dip, then shift your presentation a little bit by using big bell peppers. Cut the tops off and remove the seeds, fill the peppers with your favorite dips, and scatter the chips around the peppers on a serving platter.

LA DOLCE VITA

LA DOLCE VITA! THE ADOPTION OF THIS ITALIAN PHRASE IN THE ENGLISH LANGUAGE WAS PROMPTED BY FEDERICO FELLINI'S FILM OF THE SAME NAME RELEASED IN 1961. IT REFERS TO THE SWEET LIFE AND BRINGS IMAGES OF RELAXED AND GLAMOROUS ITALIANS LIVING LIFE TO THE FULLEST. IF THAT DOESN'T INSPIRE A CELEBRATION, I DON'T KNOW WHAT CAN! WE USED THIS IDYLLIC INSPIRATION TO CREATE AN EVENT THAT CELEBRATED LIFE AND ALL THAT WE HAVE TO BE GRATEFUL FOR. IN LIEU OF A GUEST BOOK, WE ASKED GUESTS TO WRITE DOWN WHAT THEY WERE THANKFUL FOR AND DROP IT INTO A PRETTY GLASS GRATITUDE JAR. OUR DINING TABLE WAS COVERED IN COMFORT FOODS, AND WE SET UP AN OLIVE OIL BAR SO THAT OUR GUESTS COULD EXPERIMENT WITH VARIETIES OF OLIVE OIL FLAVORS.

LA DOLCE VITA ITALIAN PUNCH

I first served this punch at an event that I co-hosted with Frangelico. They had all sorts of cocktail ideas for our Italian-themed party, and I challenged them to work with me on a recipe that would work for a punch bowl. It turned out to be a hit! We decided to add a touch of glamour by serving the mix in champagne coupes and allowing each guest to select their own garnish from a tray of rosemary, clove-studded orange slices, and sliced figs.

2 parts Frangelico

3 parts pomegranate juice

2 parts cranberry-infused Vodka (purchased or make your own)

I part lime juice

I/2 part orange juice

I/2 part honey solution (2 parts honey to I part hot water)

Clove-studded orange slices, for garnish

In a large punch bowl, mix all ingredients together in the order listed. Do not add ice to the punch bowl, but instead provide an ice bucket with finely chipped or shaved ice. Serve punch in ice-filled glasses. Garnish with clove-stuffed orange slices.

SERVES A LARGE GATHERING, ACCORDING TO AMOUNTS YOU CHOOSE

CRANBERRY-INFUSED VODKA:

Although you can buy cranberry-infused vodka, it is simple to make your own. All you need is a cup of fresh cranberries, I/3 cup of sugar, 3 of cups vodka, and I tablespoon of water. Simply dissolve the sugar in the water/cranberry mixture over high heat, then pour it into a carafe and add the vodka! This is a great make-ahead for your party planning.

VARIATION:

For an alcohol-free alternative, here are some substitutions: hazelnut or almond extract for Frangelico (use I teaspoon extract in place of every 4 tablespoons Frangelico); cranberry juice for cranberry-infused Vodka.

TRUFFLED MAC AND CHEESE

1 pound pasta, any shape

1 teaspoon garlic salt

1 teaspoon olive oil

1 cup crumbled Ritz crackers

4 tablespoons white truffle oil,
    divided

1/4 cup butter

1/4 cup freshly minced garlic

1/4 cup flour

2 cups milk

1 cup half-and-half

1 teaspoon paprika

4 ounces mascarpone cheese

8 ounces white cheddar cheese,
    grated

8 ounces mild Gouda, grated

Salt and pepper

Parmesan cheese, for topping,
    optional

Cook pasta in water according to package directions, adding a teaspoon each of garlic salt and olive oil. Drain pasta and set aside.

Toss the crumbled Ritz crackers in 1 teaspoon of truffle oil. Set aside.

In a different pot, brown the butter and minced garlic over medium heat and then whisk in the flour. Gradually whisk in the milk and half-and-half to achieve a smooth consistency. Add the paprika and mascarpone; whisk until smooth. Add the cheddar and Gouda cheeses and mix until melted. Finally, add the truffle oil and whisk. Add salt and pepper to taste.

Preheat oven to 350° F.

Add the pasta to the cheese mixture and stir to coat. Divide the prepared mixture among mini baking dishes, such as Le Creuset. Top with the truffled Ritz crackers. Sprinkle with Parmesan cheese, if using. Bake for about 25 minutes, until bubbly and golden on top.

Olive Oil Bar

If you seem to be lacking one item as you plan your party but can't put your finger on a solution, try the olive oil bar! Olive oil can enhance any flavor, especially when it has already been infused. Stock your olive oil bar with four different types of olive oil. We used lemon, basil, rosemary, and traditional; experiment with whatever your closest store has to offer.

Once you've picked your olive oils, pick your bottles to give your party some pretty styling. I use different shapes and sizes for a dynamic look.

Next, the vehicle: I recommend a variety of breads and vinegars to complement the olive oils. Slice a baguette or some ciabatta. Set up a self-serve buffet table where guests can access any accent they would like to try. Arrange along with other fillers, such as a mix of nuts or a cheese board. This is a great way to serve bread to go along with whatever is on the menu that evening.

For garnish and presentation, wrap small loaves of bread with twine and a sprig of rosemary to create a wonderful aromatic draw!

FALL FÊTE

FALL GATHERINGS AT OUR WHITE OAKS RANCH ARE
RELAXED AND CASUAL, BUT THAT DOESN'T MEAN WE
SACRIFICE ON TASTE OR STYLE. AFTER A MORNING
SPENT RIDING HORSES OR WALKING THE TRAILS, A
HEARTY LUNCH IS IN ORDER. INSTEAD OF GATHERING
AROUND THE TABLE, WE OFTEN SET UP A SMALL
BUFFET SO THAT OUR FAMILY OR GUESTS CAN GRAB
A BITE AND FIND A COMFORTABLE PLACE TO SIT BY
THE FIRE IN THE LIVING ROOM. IT IS NOTHING FUSSY,
JUST A SIMPLE SETUP THAT ALLOWS PEOPLE TO RELAX
AND PUT THEIR FEET UP AFTER AN ACTIVE MORNING.
A WARM TOMATO SOUP IS THE PERFECT COMPLEMENT
TO OUR MOSCOW MULE PUNCH, WHILE WARM BISCUITS
AND A PLATTER OF SEASONAL VEGETABLES WITH
HUMMUS FOR DIPPING SATISFY HUNGER.

MOSCOW MULE PUNCH

2 cups vodka
1 cup fresh lime juice
1 cup sparkling limeade, optional
1/2 cup simple syrup (see page 10)
2 cups sparkling mineral water (Topo Chico)
4 cups ginger beer
Fresh mint leaves, for garnish

Chill all ingredients ahead of time. Combine the liquid ingredients in a punch bowl just before serving. Make ginger beer the last liquid addition so that it will be fresh and sparkly! Garnish each cup with mint leaves before pouring.

SERVES ABOUT 8

TIPS:

• Slapping the mint will release a stronger flavor than muddling will.

• Substitute Mint Simple Syrup (see page 10) for traditional if you want a stronger mint flavor.

TOMATO BASIL SOUP

2 tablespoons butter
1/2 cup chopped onion
2 tablespoons minced garlic
2 cups fresh basil leaves, cut in chiffonade, plus more for garnish
4 cups peeled and diced fresh tomatoes
2 cans tomato soup
Chicken broth, as needed
1 cup heavy cream
Salt and pepper
Grated Parmesan, for garnish

Place butter, onion, and garlic in a pan and cook over medium heat until onions are translucent. Add basil, tomatoes, and soup and simmer for 30 minutes. In small batches, purée the simmered soup in a food processor or blender. To thin the soup, add chicken broth until it reaches desired consistency. Return to pan, reheat, and add the cream. Season with salt and pepper to taste and garnish with basil and Parmesan.

SERVES ABOUT 8

TIPS:

• Seasoned canned tomatoes can be substituted for fresh.

• The food processor step ensures a beautifully smooth soup. It is not necessary, however; if you want the tomatoes to have texture, skip this step.

• If you have a dairy sensitivity, substitute a dairy alternative for the cream. Keep in mind this will alter the flavor.

Bar Cart Punch

A bar cart is a beautiful accent to any party scheme we could draw up. It adds another "station" to a party, which prevents any one area from getting clogged. Another often overlooked use of a bar cart is to host your punch serving station. I repurposed a soup terrine for my punch bowl.

With this design, I employ the "use what you have" party mode. There really is no precision when throwing together a punch. There are abstract ideas and rules, but punch allows you the freedom to improvise and substitute. Something that cakes never allow!

So take advantage! Look in your liquor cabinet and your fridge and see what you have. (In our fridge we had orange juice, sparkling water, and lemons. In our bar area we had whiskey and a few other various liquors.) When looking through your on-hand ingredients, think "favorite cocktail." As I show throughout the book, favorite cocktails are amazing inspiration for a new punch! With our ingredients on hand, we determined we could make a Whiskey Sour Punch. So we went to town, adding in lemon flavor, our orange juice, and our liquors, and came up with this impromptu punch!

We want to inspire you to examine your ingredients, and mix and match! There is no formal recipe here, just your creativity!

ROASTED ROSEMARY CASHEWS

3 cups raw cashews
1/4 cup chopped fresh rosemary
1/4 cup brown sugar
3 tablespoons margarine, melted
1 teaspoon honey
1 tablespoon salt
2 teaspoons cayenne pepper
1 teaspoon ground black pepper

MAKES 3 CUPS

Preheat the oven to 350° F.

Spread the cashews on a baking sheet and bake for 12 minutes.

Meanwhile, combine all other ingredients in a separate bowl (choose a bowl big enough for tossing the cashews). Remove cashews from the oven and coat them thoroughly in the mixture. Pour out onto waxed paper and allow them to cool. If you are not serving immediately, store nuts in a container.

ANGEL BISCUITS

1 cup sour cream

1 cup unsalted butter

2 cups all-purpose flour, plus
   extra

1 teaspoon baking powder

1 teaspoon baking soda

2 teaspoons sea salt

MAKES 24 MINI OR 12 REGULAR

Preheat oven to 400° F. Coat mini or regular muffin pans with baking spray.

Mix all ingredients in a stand mixer until a dough forms. Add more flour as needed if the dough is too sticky to handle. Divide dough into small balls that can fit your muffin pan. Bake minis for about 12 minutes, or until cooked through. Regular size will take a little longer, up to 15 minutes.

TIP FOR FLOWERS:

You don't always need a vase for your flowers. For one event, I covered my entrance hall table in greenery, citrus, and candles and scattered a few white flowers around. The impact was dramatic as guests first arrived. Everything we used came from the supermarket but looked elegant and interesting. The candles really gave it a romantic twist, and the look was more casual that formal.

TIP FOR A BUFFET:

Place napkins between stacked buffet plates, maybe alternating colors, so it is easier for your guests to pick them up. This also prevents chipping.

FANCY WINTER GATHERING

SOMETIMES THE WINTER WEATHER AND HOLIDAY SEASON MAKES ME FEEL LIKE BEING A LITTLE MORE FANCY. I LIKE TO ADD A BIT OF SPARKLE AND A LOT OF SHINE WHEN ENTERTAINING AROUND THE HOLIDAYS. BUT FANCY DOESN'T ALWAYS MEAN FUSSY. A FESTIVE WINTER GATHERING CAN CONSIST OF A SIMPLE MENU OF A FAVORITE SPARKLING PUNCH AND AN ELEGANT CHEESE BOARD, AS LONG AS YOU REMEMBER TO BRING OUT YOUR MOST ELABORATE PUNCH BOWL AND SHINIEST CHEESE TRAY!

FESTIVE CHAMPAGNE PUNCH

1 1/2 cups pomegranate arils or
   fresh cranberries, or 10 ounces
   frozen cranberries
2/3 cup orange juice
3 cups water
2 tablespoons lemon juice
24 ounces ginger ale
1 (750 ml) bottle Champagne
Ice ring
Rosemary, for garnish, optional

SERVES AROUND 16

Freeze an ice ring (see below) of pomegranate arils or cranberries.

Combine the orange juice, water, lemon juice, ginger ale, and Champagne in a punch bowl. If you would like it a little stronger, add a second bottle of Champagne. Garnish the bowl or cups with pomegranate arils, cranberries, rosemary, seasonal fruit, or citrus slices.

TO MAKE AN ICE RING:

To keep your punch cold longer, use a large Bundt pan to make an ice ring. Add pomegranate arils, cranberries, sliced citrus or other garnishes to suit your recipe; then add water and freeze. To get the ice ring out of the Bundt pan, dip the pan for a moment in hot water or run the pan under the hot water tap for a few seconds. The ice ring will easily come out.

TIP FOR SUMMER PUNCH:

• For a summer punch, strawberries are an excellent choice!

POMANDER PUNCH

I like to serve this non-alcoholic punch at a Christmas Coffee I host annually for friends who have children born in the same year as my daughter. I started this celebration three years ago, soon after she was born, because I didn't know many other mothers with babies. I asked for introductions from other friends and now I feel I have another set of friends who celebrate the rich bond of motherhood with me every holiday season. Of course, it also gives us a chance to bond over the shared temper tantrums and other toddler behaviors that we are all experiencing!

3 cups fresh-squeezed orange
   juice
2 cups fresh-squeezed ruby red
   grapefruit juice
1/4 cup pomegranate juice
3 cups citrus soda (7-up or
   Sprite)
Orange slices, for garnish
Cinnamon sticks, for garnish

SERVES 8

Combine the juices in a large serving bowl and chill in the refrigerator for at least 1 hour. Just before serving, add the soda and float orange slices and cinnamon sticks. (My children have fun adding cloves to the edges of the orange slices.)

Pomanders or Clove-Studded Oranges

My kids love to make pomanders and I love to do it with them. This simple decorating DIY has a rich history that goes back to the Middle Ages, but in America we most commonly associate them with the natural Christmas decorations of Colonial Williamsburg. Today, my children give them a fun twist with abstract designs, and I like to write out their monograms in cloves! When we are done, we pile them up in a large dish or punch bowl and display them for all of December.

The fragrance makes the house smell like the holidays, and once they have dried up, they can be tossed into the fire for even more holiday aroma!

I like to make Pomander Packs as party favors for my Mother's Christmas Coffee event. I fill glass jars with everything needed to create a pomander and write the instructions on a tag. I love sending home a crafty project that my guests can make with their own families.

BREAKFAST ROLLS WITH CINNAMON BUTTER

2 cups milk

I/2 cup oil

I/2 cup sugar

I packet active dry yeast

5 cups flour, divided, plus extra for dusting

I teaspoon salt

Melted butter, for brushing

Sea salt, for sprinkling

Cinnamon Butter, for serving

MAKES 3 DOZEN SMALL BISCUITS

Scald the milk, oil, and sugar on medium-high heat until just before boiling. Turn off heat and let it cool. Once cooled (about an hour), add the yeast to the milk mixture and let it sit for 5 minutes. Mix in 4 cups of flour and the salt and set aside in warm place to rise for at least an hour. Dough will be sticky.

Once the dough has doubled in size, transfer it onto a floured surface. Coat the dough with the remaining 1 cup flour until it is easy to handle and the stickiness has subsided.

Preheat the oven to 350° F.

Divide dough into uniform balls about 1 1/2 inches in diameter and set side by side, touching, on an ungreased baking sheet. Brush with melted butter and sprinkle with sea salt. Bake for 10 to 15 minutes, or until slightly browned.

CINNAMON BUTTER

I/2 cup butter, softened

2 cups confectioners' sugar

I tablespoon cinnamon

I teaspoon vanilla

2 tablespoons honey

Mix all ingredients together in a stand mixer. Start on very low speed to keep the sugar from billowing out. Transfer to a serving dish accompanied by a butter knife.

TIPS:

• Make rolls ahead of time and freeze.

• This dough can also be used for pigs in a blanket or chicken biscuits.

The Art of the Cheese Board

When you have a party, yet it's not quite mealtime, what do you do? I am in love with the cheese board. It's a way I get to use my styling skills *and* feed my guests!

Let's talk about cheese board essentials. **First, select your cheeses!** I choose a soft cheese, a semi-soft cheese, and then at least one hard cheese. For explanation's sake, let's say Brie, Gouda, and aged cheddar. Go to town! Get different shapes and sizes so that you can make your board dynamic!

Next comes "the vehicle." Choose a mix of crackers or toasted bread and maybe some sweet or savory bread options to go alongside the cheeses. Arrange them artfully around the cheeses and all over the board.

After you have ensured full access to the cheeses via the vehicles, move to **the extras!** You'll want to add a sweet, a savory, and a crunchy. Depending on your crowd, you could even add a meat option. For my sweet addition, I love setting out fig butter.

It pairs perfectly with Brie and many other cheeses, so it is my sweet of choice. Beautiful grapes are an alternate sweet—they add color and go very well with cheese.

For a savory extra, pimento cheese gives a board a delightful Southern flare; it also will surprise your guests and set yours apart from a humdrum cheese tray.

For a crunchy offering, I go straight to a nut assortment. Some height for displaying this element is a nice touch. I used a martini glass!

If you've landed on meat, I defer to your judgment. Go with anything from prosciutto to grilled jalapeño sausage!

When assembling a cheese board, select the board to match the event. If it's a casual affair, a wooden cheese board adds an earthy tone and texture and is a great background for foods. If you find yourself hosting a fancier crowd, you can't go wrong with marble.

CHRISTMAS HOLIDAY BRUNCH

THE ANTICIPATION SURROUNDING CHRISTMAS IS JUST AS STRONG IN ME NOW AS IT WAS WHEN I WAS GROWING UP. I ENJOY HOLIDAY PARTIES ALL THROUGH THE SEASON, AND ON CHRISTMAS MORNING, I CAN HARDLY WAIT FOR THE CHILDREN TO WAKE AND THE FAMILY TO COME TOGETHER.

WHATEVER YOUR CHRISTMAS TRADITIONS ARE, I KNOW YOU ARE PROBABLY LOOKING FOR WAYS TO SAVE TIME. I'M ALWAYS LOOKING FOR RECIPES THAT I CAN PREPARE IN ADVANCE AND THAT ARE EASY TO SERVE DURING THE HUSTLE AND BUSTLE OF THE SEASON. FOR A BREAKFAST PARTY WITH FRIENDS, I LOVE THIS COFFEE PUNCH, WHICH IS ALMOST AS INDULGENT AS A DESSERT AND CERTAINLY SETS A FESTIVE TONE FOR THE DAY. THE CHARMING, TRADITIONAL DESIGN OF THE JULISKA COUNTRY ESTATE WINTER FROLIC PUNCH BOWL REALLY APPEALS TO ME. FOR BREAKFAST, THE OVERNIGHT OATS ARE EASY TO PREPARE AND SET OUT: SIMPLY TIE A SPOON TO THE JAR WITH A RIBBON, AND YOUR BUFFET CAN LOOK AS FESTIVE AS THE GIFTS AROUND THE TREE. FOR HOMEMADE COMFORT FOOD, NOTHING TOPS CINNAMON ROLLS SERVED IN CAST IRON.

RICH COFFEE PUNCH

2 cups sugar
I cup very strong hot coffee
2 cups half-and-half
2 cups whole milk
I/2 cup Frangelico
I teaspoon vanilla
I gallon coffee ice cream (I use Bluebell)

SERVES 30

Dissolve the sugar into the hot coffee and let it cool.

About 2 hours before the party, mix everything together except the ice cream and place in the freezer. Take out just before the party starts (or as the party is starting) and add the ice cream to the punch. The punch will be slushy and then will remain chilled from the ice cream.

TIPS:

• If you make too much, pour into ziplock bags and freeze for your next party.

• Make this recipe dairy free by switching up the creamy options.

• If you want to share it with the kids, leave out the Frangelico and add I tablespoon of hazelnut extract.

EASY COFFEE PUNCH

I cup brewed coffee, chilled
2 (48-ounce) bottles cold brew coffee with milk*
I/2 cup Frangelico
I gallon coffee-flavored ice cream (Bluebell)

MAKES I0 OR MORE MUGS

Mix the coffees and Frangelico together. Add the scoops of ice cream at the last to keep the punch cool.

*I use Califia Farms Cold Brew with Almond Milk. While they have many flavors, I am set on the espresso version. It adds an extra coffee kick!

TIPS:

• If you want to add an extra shot of caffeine to your punch, pour coffee into ice trays the night before and add a cube to the cups.

• For an afternoon treat, go heavy on the ice cream and light on the liquid—it will transform into a delicious dessert!

• To make it kid friendly, eliminate the Frangelico.

BACON AND SWISS QUICHE

2 sticks butter, softened

8 ounces cream cheese, softened

2 1/2 cups all-purpose flour

1 pound bacon, cooked and
     crumbled

3 cups Swiss cheese, shredded

1 cup chopped green onion

5 eggs, beaten

3 cups heavy cream

Salt and pepper

MAKES 15 CUPCAKE-SIZE
QUICHES

Mix butter, cream cheese, and flour together in a food processor until a ball of dough forms. Turn the dough out onto a floured surface and divide into medium-size balls to fit into a cupcake pan. Press the balls into the cupcake molds, starting in the center and working up the sides. Add more if needed to make a thick crust in the each mold.

Preheat the oven to 350° F.

Place the crumbled bacon in the bottom of the newly formed crust. Add the Swiss cheese and green onions. In a bowl, mix together the eggs and heavy cream. Add salt and pepper to taste. Pour egg mixture into the individual quiche crusts, filling three-quarters full. Bake for 35 minutes, or until set.

CAST IRON CINNAMON ROLLS

1 cup milk

1 cup sour cream

1/2 cup oil

1/2 cup sugar

1 tablespoon brandy

1 packet active dry yeast

5 cups all-purpose flour, divided, plus extra for
   dusting

1 cup melted butter

3 cups cinnamon sugar

**MAKES ENOUGH TO FILL 4 (10–12-INCH) CAST IRON
SKILLETS**

Heat the milk, sour cream, oil, and sugar in a
medium-size pan until just before boiling. Turn
mixture off and add the brandy. Let cool until
warm to the touch; then add in the yeast. Let stand
for 5 minutes.

To the milk mixture add 4 cups flour and mix
until combined. Cover the dough and let rise for
30 minutes, or until doubled in bulk. Sprinkle
remaining 1 cup flour into the risen dough, which
will be sticky; this makes it easier to handle. Then
turn the dough out onto a floured surface. Divide
dough into three parts. Preheat the oven to 350° F.

Roll out one piece of dough into a rectangular or
oval shape and then brush the entire surface with
the melted butter. Sprinkle 1 cup cinnamon sugar
on top. Starting with one of the long sides of the
rectangle, roll the dough towards the opposite side.
Once the dough is in a long roll, cut 2-inch slices
and place them side by side into a cast iron skillet
as you go. Repeat with the other portions of the
divided dough. (I suggest freezing extra rolls in
aluminum pans for a quick fix when you have last-
minute guests.) Bake for 12 minutes, or until the
rolls are baked through.

GLAZE

4 cups confectioners' sugar

1/4 cup half-and-half

1/2 cup milk

1 teaspoon clear vanilla extract

Mix all ingredients together in a stand mixer and
spread over warm rolls.

TIPS:

• Go crazy with the cinnamon sugar sprinkle—make
it more of a shower!

• Make mini cinnamon rolls for a pick-up party by
making dough rectangles less wide.

— Punch Bowl as Ice Bucket —

Another practical and pretty use for a punch bowl is as an ice bucket. Nothing says "festive" like a grand display of great Champagne! Pickard Porcelain makes a monogrammed punch bowl that I adore. It can be used for punch or flowers, piled high with ornaments or fruit, or used like I do here—as an ice bucket! Line up some flutes and let your guests serve themselves. You could surround it with caviar, chocolates, a cheese tray, or mixers for the champagne, like cranberries or orange juice.

OVERNIGHT OATS

Overnight oats are the perfect go-to when hosting a group. With all of our different taste buds and all of our dietary needs, this versatile dish can accommodate even the most challenging of diets!

1/2 cup rolled oats

2 tablespoons chia seeds

I cup milk, yogurt, or coconut milk

I teaspoon vanilla extract

Selection of add-ins: fruit, honey or other sweetener, shredded coconut, cinnamon sugar, nuts (unsalted pecans, slivered almonds, raw cashews), granola

MAKES I SERVING

For each serving, place rolled oats and chia seeds in a glass jar of your choice. Combine milk or yogurt with vanilla extract and pour over the dry mixture. Set in refrigerator overnight.

Provide plenty of optional add-ins for your guests to choose from, including some dairy-free choices.

BABY SPRINKLE

THERE IS NOTHING MORE EXCITING THAN LEARNING THAT A FRIEND IS EXPECTING A BABY. IT IS CERTAINLY AN OCCASION TO CELEBRATE! TRADITION SAYS THAT BABY SHOWERS ARE APPROPRIATE ONLY FOR FIRST-TIME MOTHERS. BUT ANY BABY IS WORTH A CELEBRATION, SO TODAY, WE OFTEN REPLACE THE "SHOWER" WITH A "SPRINKLE." EVERYTHING BUT THE NAME IS THE SAME AS A SHOWER, FROM THE GIFTS TO THE GAMES. I THINK IT MAKES THE PERFECT SETTING FOR A PUNCH THAT CAN BE EASILY SERVED TO GUESTS AS THEY MIX AND MINGLE. MANY OF TODAY'S HONOREES OPT TO SKIP THE GIFT OPENING PORTION OF THE PARTY AND SAVE THAT FOR LATER, WHICH MEANS THAT, AS A HOSTESS, YOU NEED TO COME UP WITH A FUN GAME OR ACTIVITY TO KEEP YOUR GUESTS BUSY. I LIKE TO PROVIDE A PLACE FOR GUESTS TO WRITE WORDS OF WISDOM FOR THE PARENTS-TO-BE. BE SURE TO INCLUDE SOME NON-ALCOHOLIC PUNCH FOR THE EXPECTANT MOTHERS IN ATTENDANCE (SEE ALCOHOL-FREE MILK PUNCH ON PAGE 100).

BIG MOMMA'S BRANDY ALEXANDER

My mother is famous among our friends and family for her Brandy Alexanders. They are decadent and delicious and make any occasion more festive, whether it is a summer soiree or a holiday gathering.

I cup skim milk

1/2 cup brandy

1/2 cup crème de cacao

6 scoops vanilla ice cream

Lots of ice

SERVES 6 TO 8

Combine the milk, brandy, cream de cacao, ice cream, and ice together in a blender and mix until smooth. Pour mixture into a punch bowl over ice.

ALCOHOL-FREE MILK PUNCH

3 cups whole milk

2 cups half-and-half

8 ounces simple syrup (see page 10)

I cup vanilla bean ice cream (I use Bluebell)

I tablespoon Mexican vanilla

1/4 cup vanilla extract

Sprinkle Milk Ice Cubes

Combine the milk, half-and-half, simple syrup, ice cream, and vanilla together in a pitcher and mix well. Refrigerate to chill. Place ice cubes in the punch bowl at the last minute and pour the milk punch over them.

TO MAKE SPRINKLE MILK ICE CUBES:

Pour desired colored sprinkles in the bottom of each square in your ice tray. Fill with either water or milk and freeze overnight.

TIPS:

• Do not use nonpareil sprinkles for the ice cubes. Their colors will bleed once the liquid touches them.

• Some recipes call for confectioners' sugar instead of simple syrup. I use simple syrup because it preserves the integrity of the texture of the punch instead of risking lumps in our drink.

• Pour leftover punch into freezer pop molds.

Sprinkle-Rimmed Glasses

Into two shallow dishes, pour a little honey in one and sprinkles in the other; set them next to each other. Dip the rim of each milk glass lightly into the honey and immediately into the sprinkles. Shake off any loose sprinkles, and then set the glasses right side up to dry.

ICE CREAM SANDWICHES

BEST-EVER SEA SALT CHOCOLATE CHIP COOKIES

2 sticks butter, softened

I cup white sugar

3/4 cup packed brown sugar

2 eggs

2 tablespoons vanilla extract

I teaspoon vanilla paste

3 cups all-purpose flour

I/2 teaspoon baking soda

I/2 teaspoon baking powder

I teaspoon sea salt, plus extra
    for dusting

2 cups chocolate chips

MAKES 3 DOZEN

Preheat the oven to 350° F.

Cream the butter and sugars together. Add the eggs one at a time, mixing after each addition. Mix in the vanilla extract and paste.

Combine the flour, baking soda, baking powder, and 1 teaspoon sea salt together, then add this to the moist ingredients. Lightly mix in the chocolate chips. Once the dough is mixed, use a 2 1/2-inch ice cream scoop to form uniform-sized balls, and place them on an ungreased cookie sheet about 2 inches apart. Press each ball down and sprinkle sea salt on top. Bake for 10 minutes, or until cooked through. Remove from the oven and transfer to a wire rack to cool.

TO ASSEMBLE THE SANDWICHES:

Pick your favorite ice cream flavor(s) and let it/them soften slightly. Using the same scoop you used for the cookies, place one scoop of ice cream on top of a cookie; then gently press a second cookie on top of the ice cream so it pushes out to the edge or very slightly beyond. Be careful not to break the cookies.

Roll each cookie sandwich in sprinkles, then place on a tray and freeze. When ready to serve, wrap each sandwich in waxed paper to prevent messes.

TIPS:

• Refrigerate cookie dough after scooping, before you bake, for thicker cookies.

• Do not overbake the cookies or your sandwiches will be too crispy to bite into.

A GUIDE TO GARNISHES

Instead of having to stand around the punch at your party and explain all about it, let garnishes do half of the work for you! Garnishes are a festive way to convey what is in your party punch while adding a beautiful element to each glass.

When choosing a garnish, you want to look for vibrant color and also choose something that can contribute in taste as the punch is poured over the course of the night.

Review the ingredients in your recipe. What will complement those flavors the best, and what will add that extra dash of freshness to top it off?

I suggest garnishing your glasses about 20 minutes before the guests arrive. This task can be easily delegated to that wonderful friend who is always looking for a job or a way to help!

Following is a simple guide to garnishes (this page through page 108):

CITRUS GARNISHES

Lemons and limes are going to be your go-to garnishes. Their vivid colors and wonderful tartness can break up even the sweetest of punches. Lemons and limes are truly versatile; very rarely will they throw off the flavor that you are going for. I love them in my Margarita Punch, Moscow Mule Punch, Mojito Punch, Watermelon Punch and many more!

While *oranges* can be used throughout the year, I like the mark of an orange for fall and Christmas punches. I adore using them with cloves in all of our family's Christmas punches! They also make a beautiful addition to a mimosa punch for a wedding day brunch.

HERBS AND SAVORY GARNISHES

Mint is an all-around garnish in the way that lemons and limes are. It is an essential addition to a punch like the Mojito or Moscow Mule, and mint is also a wonderful optional addition to balance out the sweetness of a punch centered around fruity ingredients. With its pungent flavor, bright color and alluring scent, it is sure to make any punch a success!

Rosemary is a trickier herb to use, but when paired correctly, it is a fantastic addition. I have fallen in love with it for my autumn punches. I sometimes tie two stems of it together to create floating wreath for my punch bowl. Rosemary is a fitting complement to lemon and other sweet acidic flavors.

Basil is similar to rosemary in the need for precision and specificity in pairings. Similar to rosemary, I suggest sticking with citrus and acidic flavors when you are first testing out basil as a garnish. Once you are comfortable with it, try mixing it up to create something like a strawberry basil drink! The aroma alone is enough to entice a party-goer to the punch bowl!

Cucumber is an innocuous, refreshing addition to any punch. When my husband and I talk about transforming our favorite cocktails to punch, cucumber is an essential ingredient. If you relish a cucumber mojito or a cucumber margarita, you will love transforming these into a punch and using summer cucumbers as your garnish!

FRUIT AND FLOWER GARNISHES

Berries in season are all in the same class, to me, when it comes to a garnish for punch. *Raspberries, blackberries, blueberries, and strawberries* each add a beautiful twist to punch and tell the guest that they are picking up a sweeter summer drink. If you happen to be throwing a baby shower, consider the idea of garnishing with a fruit color to match the gender of the baby! This adds a special touch to the theme of your party.

Peaches are a lovely way to mark the sweet season of summer. You can transform any fruit tea into punch by adding peach puree and garnishes of sliced peaches. You could also make a wonderful peach julep! Like the fruits we've already mentioned, peaches will tell your guests that this is a seasonal and special punch with a sweet summer twist.

Cherries and pomegranates are rich in color and make pretty accents to ice rings and ice cubes. While they are gorgeous in color, they do not contribute strong amounts of flavor to the punch, which makes them extremely adaptable in their use. Pomegranates and Christmas just seem like perfect counterparts.

Mango is a superb garnish and addition to the Margarita Punch. It adds a tinge of sweetness that cuts into the strength of the tequila. I suggest cutting it into slices to better accent the flavor of the punch.

Does it get any prettier than *edible flowers*? These make sweet accents in an ice ring or simply floating in the punch. Supermarkets specializing in natural foods will probably have some on hand, but for a larger array of options, I suggest ordering edible flowers from Gourmet Sweet Botanicals. Use these for a baby shower, a Southern sip and see for the new baby, or a bridal brunch!

Garnishing can be a way to set your style and make your party punch one that guests will remember for a long time.

Punch Bowl with Flowers

One of the loveliest floral arrangements I have ever come across was created by my talented friends from A2B Table for a trunk show they hosted for my line of table linens, Halo Home by KSW. Benton Weinstock and Annie Belanger Wehrle took my breath away when I walked into Benton's kitchen and saw a sink full of orange and pink roses prepped and waiting. They were beautifully arranged in an antique Rose Medallion punch bowl and placed on the buffet. They used Oasis Floral Foam and started from the inside out to make this dramatic arrangement. I snapped this picture and posted it on my Instagram right away. What a show-stopping way to use an antique punch bowl!

INDEX

Kimberly Schlegel Whitman is a lifestyle and entertaining expert. She has published seven previous books on entertaining, is a frequent guest on *Today* and other TV shows, and is co-founder of Halo Home, a line of monogrammable table linens.

METRIC CONVERSION CHART

VOLUME MEASUREMENTS		WEIGHT MEASUREMENTS		TEMPERATURE CONVERSION	
U.S.	METRIC	U.S.	METRIC	FAHRENHEIT	CELSIUS
1 teaspoon	5 ml	1/2 ounce	15 g	250	120
1 tablespoon	15 ml	1 ounce	30 g	300	150
1/4 cup	60 ml	3 ounces	90 g	325	160
1/3 cup	75 ml	4 ounces	115 g	350	180
1/2 cup	125 ml	8 ounces	225 g	375	190
2/3 cup	150 ml	12 ounces	350 g	400	200
3/4 cup	175 ml	1 pound	450 g	425	220
1 cup	250 ml	2 1/4 pounds	1 kg	450	230

ACKNOWLEDGMENTS

Justin, JR and Millie are truly patient with photo shoots and recipe experiments, and I always appreciate their ideas and enthusiasm! When Millie garnished her plastic cup of lemonade with a lemon wedge at a little friend's poolside birthday party, I could see that all of this food styling had really rubbed off on her!

My parents are always so supportive, and even as an adult I often lean on the way they make me feel like I can do anything! My siblings and extended family give me that same feeling. I would not have been able to put this book together without the help of my friends and family. Whether they tasted a recipe or took my kids out to play while I worked, I am deeply thankful for all of their help.

There is no way my punch bowl collection would be so eclectic if it weren't for my wonderful mother-in-law, Caroline Whitman, who is a master shopper online and in antique shops and vintage stores.

I was lucky to work with so many talented people on this book and wish to thank:

Janet Rice for opening up your home to us! I loved being able to photograph a celebration in front of your gorgeous hand-painted Gracie wallpaper!

Mary Love Koons for your combined talent and kindness that make you a dream to work with! I am grateful for all you did for this project and could not have done it without you.

JerSean Golatt for always being up for trying anything! Your willingness to help with every element of the project did not go unnoticed, and I am amazed at the way you made every dish look even more beautiful!

John Cain Sargent for your beautiful photos but also your smile and kind spirit, which always enhance our parties. You make all of your subjects feel so good about their photographs! We love having you as an important part of our celebrations and are grateful for the memories you capture.

Madge Baird and the Gibbs Smith team for all that you do to make my ideas come together on the pages of our books. The impact that your belief in me has made on my life cannot be measured, and I appreciate every minute of work you all put in to it. Madge, you make my words make sense and I'm grateful beyond measure.

Suzanne Droese, Kelle Knight and the Droese PR Team, I can't even tell you how much I appreciate the way you get the word out about my work. I am very grateful for the support from your amazing team and look forward to continued adventures ahead!

Taraneh Asgharian for the beautiful food styling and Xan Moore for the recipe inspiration.

Pickard China, Halo Home by KSW and Juliska for loaning me linens and punch bowls worthy of being photographed.